Words for Every Occasion

JUDITH WIBBERLEY

D&C
David and Charles

*Dedicated to COLIN, my husband,
my love, my life, my true friend and my
inspiration in life since 2 June 1968*

A DAVID & CHARLES BOOK
Copyright © David & Charles Limited 2008

David & Charles is an F+W Publications Inc.
company
4700 East Galbraith Road
Cincinnati, OH 45236

Text copyright © Judith Wibberley 2008
Layout and Illustrations copyright
© David and Charles 2008

Printed in the USA

ISBN-13: 978-0-7153-2934-4 hardback

Commissioning Editor: Bethany Dymond
Assistant Editor: Sarah Wedlake
Designer and Illustrator: Mia Farrant
Project Editor: Natasha Reed
Production Controller: Kelly Smith
Indexer: Joan Gubbin

Contents

Acknowledgments

With special thanks to my friends Jane Trollope and Bethany Dymond at David & Charles publishers who believed in me the first time and who asked me to write this second book of original verses for crafters. Also to the team who put these lovely books together. My heartfelt thanks to those who loved the first one so much that you made this second one possible for me, and a special mention to Hilda Wibberley, my mother-in-law, who taught me how to make beautiful hand-made cards and took me into the crafting world.

My love, as always, to my husband Colin, my knight in shining armour, who fills my life with so much joy, with inspiration, support and love. All of this, and more, is also provided by my daughter Deborah who was my proofreader again, my son James, my daughter-in-law Angela, my lovely grandson Luke and his sister, my beautiful granddaughter Katie. May they always know that I love them more than any of my words could ever convey.

These verses also owe much to those who I have loved and lost but moreover to those who have been exceptional friends throughout my life, and to true angels who have touched my life in so many ways and walked with me. True friendship is such a precious gift from God and I thank Him for colouring my life with a beautiful rainbow of friends who brought me love.

In loving memory of my mother
JOAN MARY BURGESS (1925-2007)

Introduction

Words can touch us in many ways. A thoughtful card can mean as much as the touch of a hand or a smile. Special words of congratulations, love and friendship cost little yet they mean so much, for they warm the heart and comfort the soul.

This collection of celebratory verses, sayings and sentiments is invaluable for makers of greetings cards and papercraft projects. Covering every occasion, including birthdays, anniversaries, new baby, Christmas, Easter, Valentine's Day and many more, the verses range from the heartfelt to the humorous. Simply go to the relevant celebration and find the verse you most identify with. There is also a range of copyright-free motifs to allow you to decorate your projects with the perfect illustrations.

May these words bring happiness and joy into your life and may you use them in such a way that they echo around the world, making people smile because they know that they are truly loved and in the thoughts of caring friends and family.

> "*K*ind words can be short and easy to speak, but their echoes are truly endless."
> *Mother Teresa (1910–1997)*

Love is All Around

Heartfelt wishes and loving kisses
Are well and truly sent your way
Just to let you know I love you so
On this, our first Valentine's Day

Don't know what it is about you
Makes me come back for more
If I tell you it's a window
You'd say it was a door
I know it's black you tell me
I really think it's white
You drive me to distraction
But somehow it all feels right
We're chalk and cheese to others
But it seems to suit us fine
So I hope for once that you agree
And be my darling Valentine

Love is All Around
Love is All Around
Love is All Around

9

My thoughts start to wander
My poor heart skips a beat
You're so near I can feel you
Almost the time when we meet

Do I look sweet and sassy?
Will you want to be mine?
Are these earrings too brassy?
For seeing my dear Valentine

I can hear a car revving
And a horn starts to blare
As I look into the mirror
At my clothes and my hair

Well it's too late for changing
So I will just have to do
Oh please make him like me
And see this date through

Just to say...
Everything about you
is so special

Valentine's Day

Now and forever, I will be your man
For you are such a very special woman

Will you be my Valentine
And make my day complete
Because I love you very much
You just knock me off my feet

Tip
This verse is shaped for a cut-out card effect.

My
Darling Valentine
How much I love you so
This card is filled with love
From me I thought you'd like to know

Love is All Around
Love is All Around

Some words on your engagement

As you go down on bended knee
Your young lady you should woo
With love that she can clearly see
So she will smile and say 'I do'
Sweep her up into your arms
With sweet kisses that do linger
Then whilst she is recovering
Slip that ring upon her finger

You two were made for each other
What lovely news, an engagement

Congratulations

Amazing what the day can bring
A handsome man with a golden ring
So glad you two have set the date
An engagement – time to celebrate

I pray that you are the one
That I will build my home with
The one who will share my life
And hopefully in time my darling
If fate should grant my dearest wish
That you will become my wife

Wonderful news, engaged you two
My love and good wishes
in all that you do

A short engagement before the big day
How truly wonderful, what more can I say
Than here's to a couple so deeply in love
I can hear angels rejoicing in heaven above

My heartfelt congratulations on the great news

Excited to hear all the wonderful news
Wedding bells on the horizon
See you at the engagement party
So happy for you both

This engagement
present is a token
of your love for each
other, of words spoken
May it be part of your
home you build together
As the vows you will
make bind you forever

Just to say...
Congratulations on
your engagement
You are a
perfect match

Love is All Around

Love is All Around

She's only gone and done it
We all told her not to do it
My, she's gone and done it
She must be off her head

So now we'll have to do it
We will really have to do it
In proper style we'll do it
Now that she's getting wed

The hen night will be wicked
So you naughty little devils
All get dressed accordingly
The theme for this is RED

WARNING
This is no party for chickens
Only full grown hens
Looking for something
Good to crow about

Tip
This can be changed to stags, as appropriate.

Want a good reason
To let your hair down
And go wild in public?
Then look no further
HEN PARTY INVITE

STAG PARTY
INVITATION
I could write a soppy rhyme
But all of us are men
So here's the date and time
I hope to see you then

HEN PARTY INVITE
Come all you bunnies
Come with me to play
Come make me ready
Come my wedding day

Tip
The theme
of bunnies can
be changed to
angels, fairies
and so on.

May your Wedding Day
Be so very special

Hold on to your memories
Keep them in your heart
Treasure every moment
May you never ever part

You're two lovely people
So deeply in love
Made for each other
In a heaven above
Friendship to courtship,
A love ever true
Commitment forever,
Celebrations now due

May you always be as close as you are today
And may your partnership blossom
In a home filled with love

As you take on this commitment
Hold each other close and say
All the words you will remember
Forever and a day

May your life be blessed with sunshine
That shines down from above
With rainbows to surround you
In a circle made of love

As you stand before Him as man and wife
Know that He will bless you both
With many things in life
And walk with you
Always

Just to say...
Though I can't share the celebrations in person, you are in my thoughts

Love is All Around
Love is All Around

Love is a precious gift from God
As you stand before Him together
As man and as wife promise Him
That you will treasure it always
CONGRATULATIONS

As you take on this commitment
May the love you feel today grow
As the years pass, the seasons change
And life takes on a new meaning
As you become man and wife

Tip
You can change line five to alter man and wife to partners.

May your
Wedding Day
Be all you
dreamed of
With wonderful
memories
All wrapped up
in love

To the Bride and Groom
Take each precious moment
Of this, your Wedding Day
Remember them forever
May they never fade away

Marriage is so special, for you
do not marry someone you can live with,
you marry someone you cannot live without

Love is All Around

Love is All Around

21

May your
Wedding Day be
wonderful

Filled with
family and
friends

For our beautiful bridesmaid
The day would not be the same
Without your love and kindness
Making it so special for us both

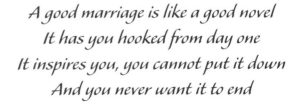

A good marriage is like a good novel
It has you hooked from day one
It inspires you, you cannot put it down
And you never want it to end

You make the perfect couple
May this day be the beginning
Of something so wonderful
That you never want it to end

Just to say...
Heartfelt congratulations
to you both
On your Wedding
Day

Marriage is like a work of art
With dedication, passion, patience
And conviction you can create
Something truly priceless

Love is All Around

Love is All Around

Feel our love
LOVELOVELOVELOVELOVE
As you walk down the aisle
To smile and say that you do
Know that our hearts are filled
With sweet memories of you
LOVELOVELOVELOVELOVE
The child we held so closely
Who captivated us so
Our girl we love
A time to go
LOVELOVE
LOVE

Tip
This verse can be used in a heart-shaped card.

Our Beautiful Daughter,
on her Wedding Day

So beautiful in body, mind and spirit
May you shine on your wedding day
As brightly as you have always done
Since the day you first smiled at us

Never thought that anyone
Would capture your heart
But when the love bug came
We could tell from the start
That everything changed
When she smiled at you
Good on you mate
Congratulations
To both of you
CHEERS
W
E
D
D
I
N
G
WISHES

We both want to thank you so much
When it comes to being a Best Man
We think you're definitely the best
Without you there our special day
Would not have been as special
THANK YOU FOR YOUR
THOUGHTFULNESS

Love is All Around
Love is All Around

As you know I'm not very good with words
But then again you can't have everything
Enjoy the gift that comes with my love
HAPPY ANNIVERSARY

Just to say...
The past year has
been heaven
I am so glad
we met

Mum & Dad

Your love for
each other is an
inspiration

That colours our
lives with hope

And makes our
dreams

Always come true

You lighten the burden
Life sometimes puts on me
Without your loving smile
And kindness I would be
In a world far less exciting
In a home without a heart
You colour days together
I hope that we never part

This comes with loving wishes
On your Anniversary day
For a couple who are dearer
Than words could ever say

Love is All Around

Love is All Around

There is not a card big enough
To fill with all my love for you
Even the biggest box they make
Has not the space for kisses due
So I've zipped them very carefully
In a special email so you will find
Waiting for when you log on again
A loving virus of a very special kind

Just to say...
You make every
day special,
Not just our
anniversaries

Happy Anniversary, my Dearest Husband
Each year spent with you is more
Wonderful that the one before
I love growing more in love with you
And the crazy little things you do

My Darling Husband
Sometimes it's hard to find
The exact words to tell you
How much you mean to me
So sometimes I don't say
Anything at all and hope
Somehow you understand
But on this special day
I just want to tell you
Each passing day
I love you more
And more
MY LOVE

To my Wonderful Wife

The special bond of our love
Gives me the strength
To move mountains

Love is All Around
Love is All Around

My last twelve months
Have been so magical
Happy Anniversary
My love, my life
My darling
Wife

*Y*our 4th anniversary
Has just come your way
So celebrate with silk gifts
On this joyous day

Tip
Change the
year and replace
with the
appropriate
gift.

On our 5th Wedding Anniversary
Thanks for all the love you give
All the caring things you do
The fun we both have together
Dreams you've made come true

On the 10th Anniversary
Of the lovely day we wed
There aren't many words
I have not already said
All the sharing and caring
Having you so close to me
These are the special things
They mean the world to me

May this Silver Anniversary Day
Bring together a collection
Of beautiful memories
And create dreams of
More precious tomorrows

For two lovely people
This card comes to say
May love and joy be yours
On your special
Ruby Wedding Day

On Our 35th Wedding Anniversary

People say that I'm so lucky,
And this is so very true
For my luck began the day
That I fell in love with you

I felt a kind of magic
Like an angel from above
Being sent to walk here with me
To fill my life with love

Thirty-five years gone so quickly
No longer kids, we're getting old
Many years of love ahead of us
Before they all turn to gold

But inside I'm still the young girl
You met so many years ago
And you're my handsome knight
In shining armour and I truly love you so

My love we have
So many memories to share
Treasure every one of them now
As we stand together as always
With our children, grandchildren
And great grandchildren near
On our Golden Anniversary
Fifty golden years of
LOVE

From all of us, to both of you
Our sincere joy and admiration
For showing us how love can be
On your 60th wedding celebration
Without you both to guide us on
The life we have would not be
As full of treasured memories
Of such a wonderful family

Happy 60th Anniversary

Tip
This verse can be adapted to 50th for a Golden wedding anniversary.

Baby
Joy

BABY SHOWER

Have you heard the lovely news
I have a bundle on the way
Come celebrate, my lovely mate
On my baby shower day

BABY SHOWER

Bootees and bonnets
Warm woolly blankets
Soft teddies, rattling toys
Come shower the baby
A boy, or girl maybe
Make a baby shower
Full of great joys

Just to say...
Your baby scan
looks lovely
Congratulations

Baby Joy

Baby Joy

Nappies and bottles, dummies too
Just heard congratulations are now due
Because you have a baby on the way
Love and laughter is not so far away

Your life will never ever be the same
Soon you will have a treasure to love
A special person to take your name
Sent down to you from God above

Congratulations

Just heard the wonderful news
How lovely, a baby on the way
You really are both so lucky
It really made my day

I take our baby in
my arms
And know what
God gave to us
When he gave us
the gift of a smile

Just to say...
A new addition to your
family
How wonderful

So glad that your little bundle
Arrived here so safe and sound
Take every day and treasure it
Golden days will now be found

Baby Joy

Baby Joy

Baby Joy

There goes a good night's sleep
Believe me though, it's well worth it
Many happy family days to you all

Bless your newborn child

Blessings be upon you all
At this truly magical time
When you celebrate
The miracle
Of new
Life

A baby is a blessing in life Make every day count

Congratulations

On the birth of your first child
They say that the first
Twenty years are the worst
After that you usually
Start losing your memory

Welcome to the world
So beautiful and new
May angels protect
And watch over you

Baby Joy

O
So
perfectly
beautiful
in every way
BABY CUDDLES
BABY GIGGLES
BABY RATTLES
BABY PHOTOS
BABY BOOTEES
BABY DIAPERS
BABY BOTTLES

Tiny fingers, tiny feet
A miracle in every way
A joy to hold, a life unfolds
On this very special day

Perfect little fingers
Tiny feet with little toes
Twinkling eyes like stars
And a little button nose

Heard you were now
The proud parents of four
You will need a new house
If you want any more

Congratulations on becoming an Auntie
Think of all that babysitting money

Baby Joy

Baby Joy

41

A child in the house
Brings a reason for living
Purpose to each day
And joy beyond compare
CONGRATULATIONS

I look at her tiny face
My heart just sings
Your daughter's an angel
Without any wings

A daughter, how
wonderful
Girls are so gorgeous
In pink, frills and lace
With butterfly eyelashes
And a beautiful face

A son, how wonderful
Boys are so charming
Always smiling at you
With eyes that watch
Everything you do

Treasure all the
Little moments of joy
Congratulations on the birth
Of your darling
Little boy

One   Two
Three four five six seven
Eight nine ten eleven twelve
Thirteen fourteen fifteen sixteen
Seventeen eighteen nineteen twenty
Two one – twenty one – time flies
Capture every moment
Keep them in your
Heart

Baby Joy

Baby Joy

Baby Joy

So much pink, I must be seeing double
Look out Mum and Dad two girls, double trouble
You might need a new bathroom, mirrors on the wall
For in a few more years you won't get in there at all
Twin girls you are so lucky, think of all the joys
That is until their friends all turn out to be boys

Congratulations
On the birth of your lovely twins
Two sweet bundles of joy
A beautiful girl and a handsome boy

Just to say...
What a lovely family
of four, with two
babies to adore

Twins

Twice the nappies, twice the fun
So happy for your new family
Welcome to your daughter
And also to your son

Tip
Change the verse,
depending on the sex
of the children. E.g. for
one of each, it would
be '...think of all the
joy, a beautiful girl, a
handsome boy'.

Congratulations are overdue
For a beautiful baby times by two
Twins how adorable, double joys
Lucky parents, lucky boys

CONGRATULATIONS ON THE
BOYS' ARRIVAL

Baby Joy of Baby Joy

Three babies all in a row
Each one so charming
And all waiting to grow
Into beautiful children
Of a proud dad and mum
Two beautiful daughters
A handsome young son
Our love goes to you all
Congratulations are due
May angels watch over
Everything that you do

Tip
This verse can be altered to suit the babies born.

Adorable faces, angels with curls
From now on it's
GIRLS – GIRLS– GIRLS

May your lovely daughters
Be three times a lady

Congratulations
Congratulations
Congratulations
Three adorable bundles of joy
Boy, oh boy, oh boy!

A blessing be upon
Your family and newborn children

My heart was lost to her
The moment I looked into those eyes
She is so precious to me
My darling baby girl

WELL DONE MUM

Tip
Change the
gender of
the baby as
appropriate.

On the birth of
our first child

My Darling
I believe in angels
For in her face I see
Our love looking
Back at me

Well Done Mum

My darling wife
You have brought love
Into my life, and a joy
I never knew existed
Until I held our child
In my arms and saw
All of our dreams
Become a reality

Glad to hear that all went well
That giving birth was fun
Get all then rest you can now
Sleepless nights have just begun

Just to say...
A baby is wonderful,
marvellous and
beautiful
Congratulations

Baby Joy

Child of your child, love of your love
Joy of your joy, life of your life
A grandchild captures your heart
And brings joy into your life
CONGRATULATIONS
To the proud Grandparents

Congratulations on your
NEW GRANDCHILD
Wishing you all the pleasures
Of your new role as grandparents
Heart-warming moments to treasure
A world of discoveries and happiness

New Grandchild

Today is so very special
Your smile lights up our day
You are so very lovely
In every kind of way
We are both so very happy
Your life here has begun
Know you are so precious
Our darling baby grandson

*C*ongratulations
You were ideal parents
and you will be
perfect grandparents

To a brand new set of Grandparents
May .... bring you both
All the very special joy and love

Tip
Insert the name of the new grandchild.

Baby Joy

Baby Joy

May God bless your little one
On this special Christening Day

Feel the love of the Lord
Wrapping itself around you
As you lovingly bring to Him
Your new child and family
To receive His blessings
On this special day

Praise His name and ask for His love
On this most joyous of occasions
The Christening Day
Of your most precious child

May this special day be filled with joy
To welcome here your little boy
As one and all bow down before
A loving God whom we adore
To bless this child and name him too
Before Our Lord who's always true

A life so precious, A gift from God
A Godparent For our child
Another gift From God
Bless you

May the angels sing in heaven
To welcome your new arrival
Into the house of the Lord
This special Christening Day

Baby Joy

53

Two beautiful children
A loving wife that I adore
Such a wonderful feeling
I could not ask for more

Yet God has sent another
Angel into our loving care
Each day is so very special
Just knowing she is there

Come join our lovely family
As we thank the Lord today
For life and love He gives us
As He guides us on our way

May you feel the love
Of your family and friends
As you celebrate today
The blessing of your
Beautiful child

Just to say...
The door is always
open, all you need
to do is call on
Him

One God
Who loves all of His children
And sends us His angels to love
Praise His name as you ask
Him to bless your child
And walk with her
Through life
Forever
Near
By

Blessings to you
And your bouncy
Little Bundle of Joy

*M*ay all the love in the world
Surround your new family
On this special day

Baby Joy

55

Happy Birthday

May the house become alive with
Laughter, fun and happiness
As you party with your friends
And celebrate your birthday

Slow down and take it easy
You deserve the best they say
So relax and reflect on life around
Because today is your birthday

Birthdays are a time
To reflect on the past year
And to celebrate the one ahead
To look closely at life itself
And to thank God for all we have

You become more beautiful
With each passing year
God bless you so
On your birthday

Just to say...
Of all the cards in
the world, this one
contains the
most love

On your birthday
May the love and joy
That you give to others
Be returned to you tenfold

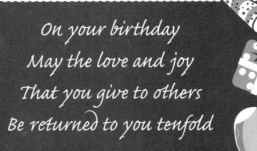

On paper you might be
Getting old
But in your heart
You are forever young

Remember, we were young once
Well I think we both were
I Forget things sometimes
But never your
BIRTHDAY

*M*ay love, peace and joy
Surround you on the day
You celebrate your birth

Happy Birthday Happy Birthday

The years have been kind to you
How fortunate at your age

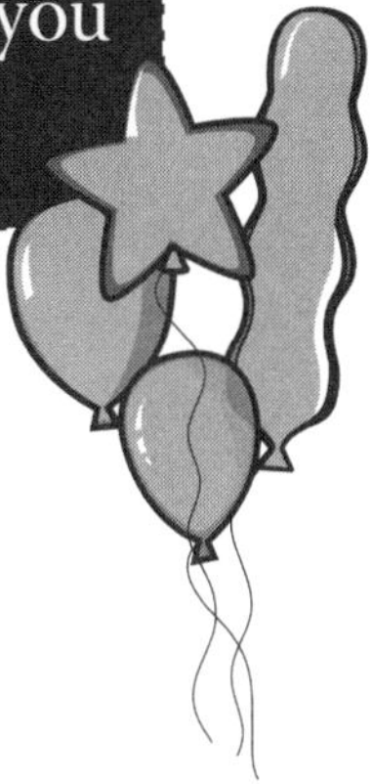

I was going to put
Money inside your card
But it is your birthday
So I surprised you
And left it out

Sending this great card to
my very best mate
Get on your glad rags it's
time to celebrate

Be in the moment
Enjoy your birthday
Be happy today
And always

I thought about a soppy card

And then I changed my mind

Just sending special wishes

To show you are in mind

I would normally text but

at this time of year

tradition dictates

cards are sent

so here it is

a card

HBTU

X

Happy Birthday

Happy Birthday

Hope everything
In your garden is rosy
And calm on this very
Special Birthday

You are old enough to get away with it
And young enough to enjoy it
So let your hair down
And celebrate
In style

My
dear friend
On your birthday
I donated your present
to a deserving charity
They said to tell you
that the champagne
was a little warm
but it helped
to wash
down
the
big
box
of
chocolates
HAPPY
BIRTHDAY

Another year to be
thankful

For all the love God gives

On your birthday look
around you

And Know He truly lives

Happy Birthday

Happy Birthday

The postman is here knocking
As it's birthday time today
For an extra special one year old
Whose friends have come to play

HAPPY FIRST BIRTHDAY

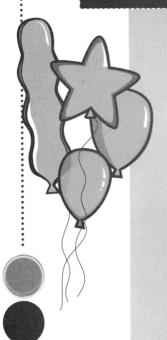

For a cheeky little boy
Who is two today
May lots of adventures
Come bouncing your way

How big are you
Not three today
Well goodness me
Hip, hip, hurray!

There is someone knocking
at your door
With birthday cards
because today
YOU ARE FOUR

One, two, three, four, five
Candles burning in a row
A birthday wish, a loving kiss
You are a special child to know

Goodness me six years old
Then you don't need to be told
How to blow those candles out
You've done this before without a doubt

A grown-up girl who is seven
A little angel truly sent from heaven
May your day be as lovely as you
Have fun in all that you do

I heard that it's your birthday
They tell me that you are eight
Hope you have a jolly time
When you go out to celebrate

Nine years old today
Hope that the day brings you
All things good and mates
To share the moment with

*H*ope you have so much fun
Now you are ten
That you can't wait for next year
To do it all again

Coming of Age

Today is the beginning
Of the countdown to
The day we get sole control
Of the bathroom again

18

Every good wish
On your special birthday
All the best for the future
May every plan you make
Work out the way you want it to

Tip
This verse is
shaped like a
birthday cake – the
number can be
altered for any
age.

21st

Childhood dreams can now come true
As you start on your way
Along life's busy, winding road
It all starts from today
The day the boy becomes a man
And dons a cloak of dreams
Keep reaching for those stars you seek
They are nearer than they seem

CONGRATULATIONS AS YOU COME OF AGE

Tip
This verse suitable for an 18th birthday, just change the number at the top.

If 30 is a big number
You just can't handle
Think of being 21 again
With 9 years' experience

NAUGHTY 40 TODAY
How much fun we can have
Now you have reached forty
We can party all night long
Go out and be so naughty

50 TODAY
If you had scored that at cricket
You would be a sporting hero
But then to me you truly are
A hero and a great sport every day

60th Birthday
First we will light the candles
Then I will call for the fire brigade

70 TODAY

Enjoy your 70th birthday all day long
But when the day has gone
May the wishes sent, the love bestowed
And the memories linger on

80 TODAY

There is a calm serenity behind your smiling eyes
A beauty time has given you, so gentle and so wise
Eighty years of wisdom behind the words you say
May love and joy surround you upon this special day

90

For everything you mean to us, for each and every day
Of love and guidance you have shown to help us make our way
For each and every moment, for every single kiss
Your birthday is so precious that we wouldn't want to miss
Telling you how much you're loved and treasured every day
Hope this day is magical in every kind of way

My how times have changed
In the past 100 years
But you have remained
the same
As wonderful as ever

Tip
The age can
be changed for
others such as
70, 80, 90 and
so on.

Happy Birthday

71

I hope today's the kind of day
To make you smile out loud
That brings out rays of sunshine
From behind a lonely cloud
The kind of day that's special
Is what I now wish for you
My dearest, darling husband
With all my love and kisses too

Though we can't be together
On your birthday celebration
You are always in my thoughts
Whatever the occasion

Hope your day is filled with joy
For you deserve the best
So get dressed up and smile
Whilst others do the rest

CONGRATULATIONS

Another year, why
should we worry
There's nowhere to
go in any hurry
We are together in
favourite places
Memories etched
upon our faces
Hand in hand we
go through life
A lucky man and
his lovely wife

*HAPPY
BIRTHDAY MY
DARLING*

Tip

This could also
be an anniversary
verse, by changing
the word birthday
to anniversary.

How could I forget
Your birthday

DAD

The day they
Broke the mould

BROTHERS
Are sent to us
So our lives will be interesting
And you certainly live up to
That expectation

It's great to watch a football match
You can cheer your team along
Enjoy the match on your birthday
Those tickets cost me a song

A LOVELY GRANDSON

Your lovely smile that warms my heart
A laugh that brings me joy
I fell for your charms from the start
Grandma's darling little boy
May God protect you in every way
In everything you say and do
Especially on this special day
When I send birthday love to you

Son, you are so special
so we want you to know
We treasure every moment
as we watch you grow
HAVE A GREAT BIRTHDAY

Mummy
This card comes to tell you
That I really love you so
For caring so much for me
And helping me to grow

HAPPY BIRTHDAY SISTER

I
Do
Love you, so
For your birthday
I ordered you chocolates
Clothes, perfume and wine
You really should not leave
Your card next to the computer!

*T*o a Dear Aunt
Who looks younger than I do
Have an extra-special
Birthday

To a Dear Daughter

God bless you on this special day
For your precious love, for being you
No parent could ask for more

For a Sweet Granddaughter

I'm sending this card
With love and good wishes
Wrapped in my cuddles and kisses
To a sweet little girl on this, your big day
From a Grandma so proud that she can say
You're a lovely granddaughter, a joy to behold
Enjoy your big day now that you're four years old

Granddads are special
God made them just to be
The one who will let you
Sit high upon their knee

When you have a worry
You cannot tell another
Something for him to hear
And not tell your mother

He will tell you clearly
Just what you should do
Make everything right
Because he loves you

Granddads have birthdays
But they never grow old
They are special treasures
Worth more than gold

You are such a special lady
A Gran without compare
So I'm sending you my love
To tell you how much I care
You are always there to talk to
To put the world in place
I always love to hug and kiss you
To see a smile upon your face

You are such a lovely neighbour
A friend way beyond compare
Each morning my life is happier
Just knowing you are there
Hope your birthday is as lovely
As you are, my dear friend

Just to say...
Friends are the best
gifts of all

There is not enough space in this card
To tell you how much I value your friendship
So I will just wish you the happiest birthday ever
And look forward to many more of them together

Happy Birthday

SURPRISE PARTY

We know she said not to bother,
She said "Please don't make a fuss"
But with a party we plan to
surprise her...
So let's hope to our plans
she remains oblivious!

Tip
This can be amended for a male.

Come to our party
It's all fancy dress
Get out glad rags
Dress to impress
Come as anyone
That we all know
Have a good time
Please don't say no

Don't tell him if you see him
For this is a great surprise
We need to get friends together
He will not believe his eyes
Next year he will be forty
A year that we all dread
So, we thought, surprise him
Celebrate 39 years instead

It's ....'s Birthday Party
Get out the streamers
Fill glasses to the brim
Celebrate birthday wishes
Especially for him

Tip
Insert the name of the birthday boy.

Pastures New

A place in the country
Somewhere you can find
All the beauty of nature
That God created for us all
Hope your move goes well
And that peace and happiness
Are your fireside companions

May each passing year
In your new house
Make it into
A home

Hope the move goes well
And that fortune brings you
Many happy days ahead
In your first new home

As soon as we saw it
We knew that it was you
Your new home is delightful
Congratulations are now due

To Mum & Dad

Thank You
For everything you do
For love and support
For being you
For each moment spent
For each precious day
For helping me
As I move away
To a place of my own
I will fill with love
With thoughts of you both
And the Lord above

With Love

May the child inside
Enjoy all the fun
Of a new home abroad
A place in the sun

New Home

A new house for you
One out in the sun
Good luck as you leave
A new life has begun

Without people like you
A house is not a home
With you living here
Colour fills the room
So laughter echoes
Welcome friend
May every day
Be happy

God Bless
Your new home
May new friends
Come to your door
Filling it with love
And laughter
Always

Pastures New
Pastures New

> *M*ay good fortune
> Move into your new home
> And may it never leave you

Builders make a house
People make it a home
May friends bring love
Colour and warmth
So that you are
happy there
always

A new house for you

Away from people you know

We wish you good fortune

But regret you must go

Take our best wishes

As you move far away

Come back and see us

Brighten up our day

New Home

A new place of your own
First time buyer for you
My how you have grown
Celebrations are due

A new place to live
How lovely for you
With lots of new friends
And new things to do
I've got the address
Soon I will call round
Now that I know, friend
Where you can be found

Pastures New

Congratulations
A new job for you
Going up in the world
Well that's long overdue
Here's to the future
May it be bright
Enjoy the rich rewards
Now the time's right

So glad you got your new job
You deserve it, my lovely friend
Knew fortune would reward you
That you would get it in the end

New Job

The time has come
For you to move on
Take another step
On the ladder
Of life
Enjoy
New things
In your new job
CONGRATULATIONS

Just to say...
May you shine every
day in your new job

There could not have been another
Good enough to fill that space
Glad you got the great new job
That it put a smile upon your face

Pastures New
Pastures New

For a really special person, with love

Drink from the cup
Of life and find all that
You desire in your quest
To shine in all you do
Be true to yourself
And you will
Always
Be

A

SPECIAL PERSON

They say the higher you go
The less hard work you do
So this step up the ladder
Will be just the job for you

A new job, that is brilliant
Knew that you would glow
You are such a lovely star
A special person to know
Well done – they are lucky
I knew that it would be 'yes'
They have recognised a talent
That only you possess

A new beginning for you
What wonderful news
We hope that it brings
Good luck and fortune
Knocking at your door

A journey starts with a single step
May God walk every one of them
To guide and protect you
BON VOYAGE

We have travelled many roads together
You are such a true and valued friend
May you find happiness in your travels
New experiences and adventures ahead
Remember me always as you journey on
For you will always be there in my heart

Bon Voyage

Perhaps we will meet again
Until then, stay well friend
As you journey on in life
You will be missed here
More than you know

With many miles between us that keep us far apart

I must keep you, darling son, close by within my heart

Just to say...

As you move away take
note of where you go
So you can come back
to visit us often

Standing on a sandy shore looking out to sea
Each wave that breaks beneath my feet
Brings back smiles at your memory
May God protect you on your travels
And bring you safe back home to me

ACROSS THE MILES

I just want to let you know
That I think of you each day
I long to hold you in my arms
Hope that time's not far away

As you move away to a place in the sun
Treasure your old life, though a new one's begun
Send us a postcard to say how you are
You are close to our hearts though you go so far

Take with you our wishes
On this day you leave
The future is attainable
If only you believe

Just to say...
As you move away to
pastures new
We are going to
miss you

As you travel the world finding new places
Remember to capture each moment, all faces
For adventures like this are always so rare
So soak up the atmosphere when you are there
And we will wait here so that wherever you roam
With hearts filled with love we will welcome you home

Pastures New
Pastures New
Pastures New

All of those things you put to one side
When there was no time, permission denied
All of those tasks you can do one by one
Retirement is here now, working has gone
Each day that you wake begins life anew
Filled with excitement and joy just for you
All of your life you have worked for this day
On this new path, may good luck light the way

Congratulations on your retirement

Switch off the alarm before it's due
Tomorrow you can relax and just rest
For the days now before you
Will be the very best

Time to retire from the daily race
To sit and relax, a smile on your face
Thinking of all that you want to do
With a new kind of life, well overdue

*C*ongratulations on your retirement
May you enjoy the rich tapestry of life
In all that you do in the future

When you go to bed tonight
Set your alarm for a lie in
Don't worry about all of us
As your leisure days begin
Be glad you are in retirement
One of those lucky people who
Makes time to take enjoyment
From everything you do

Pastures New

No more deciding what to wear for your meetings
Or sending out hundreds of company greetings
No long letters to write or formal replies
Or freshly ironed shirts with company ties
No listening to all those dull presentations
Or trying to live up to wild expectations
No stressful encounters, no watching figures
Or trying to ignore competitor's sniggers
No wondering where the time goes in life
Or explaining why you are late to the wife
No wonder retirement is a new life ahead
Or would you prefer the rat race instead
No excuses for having a smile on your face
Or for walking so proudly out of this place

Needles clicking, stitches ripping
Fabric and lace all over the place
The time is here, so all give cheer
See that smile upon her face

Coffee morning, new day dawning
No stress, no strain sat on the train
Creative flow, how time will go
Life will never be the same

Retirement days, a sunny haze
Time to walk and look at life
Look and learn, tables turn
Every day is a new adventure

The nineteenth is beckoning,
so don't be late
To tell all those golfers to
make it a date
Retirement at last, all
commitments are gone
Except to get practice for
your hole in one

*R*etirement is life's reward
For a job well done

Retirement has arrived for you
Forget computers, phone and fax
Turn your fingers green instead
Enjoy your gardening and relax

Wishing you the best of all that life
Brings your way in retirement
For you deserve days filled with
Good fortune and adventure

So far away and then so near
Retirement date is nearly here
A time to say, come join your mates
Help a good friend as she celebrates
A life of working long and hard
The details are inside this card

Retirement

FUNNY
They told me
Humour they said
He's leaving today
Things will feel dead
He made us all laugh
And working was fun
But today is the day
That he's moving on
He brought us all joy
So what should we say
He's left us speechless
We wish he would stay
But a tradition dictates
Three cheers are at hand
For a man who is magic
Champion and grand
WE WILL ALL MISS YOU

Tip
This verse can be changed for a female, and could also be used for a new job card.

In your Retirement

Treasure all the leisure days
Heading your way
You have earned them all

Pastures New
Pastures New
Pastures New

Congratulations

1st

Well Done

Enclosed is a token
Just to wish you well
Buy something grand

Tip
These are
words for a gift
card containing
money.

Nothing in life worth having comes easy
For if it did we would not value it
So pleased, well done at having achieved
Such a very special result for you to treasure
You deserve the best life has to offer you
For all of your hard work and dedication

Congratulations

Congratulations

103

We always knew that you would do it
We said you would get through it
You put all the hard work in it
You got the results from it
We send you our congratulations

Well Done

The rest were just outclassed
You were truly great
Just knew you had passed

You have done the work
Skilfully passed the test
And reached the standard
Now the hard work begins
Good luck for the future
For you deserve the best

So pleased to hear
your good news
We knew you
would win through
Our heartfelt
congratulations
Are sent today
to you

Congratulations
Hope the celebrations
Go on into the night
Knew it would all
Turn out right
WELL DONE

Nothing worth having
Is that easy to attain
All your hard work
Has really paid off

Promotion, how exciting
New challenges for you
Hope you are successful
In everything that you do

Your new promotion
Will not affect our friendship
As long as you still
Make my morning coffee
Well Done Friend

Hard work now rewarded, worth the midnight hour
To sit behind that big desk, wielding all the power
You saw the path and took it all the way to the chair
May fortune sit beside you to give you comfort there

Always knew you were special
Well done, it was long overdue
You deserve to be at the helm
Promotion will suit you

Promotion at last
I told you the best man
For the job was a woman
Well done, you

Now I know why I always liked you
I knew one day you would be the boss
Congratulations

Congratulations
Congratulations

An acting part in London
Life will never be the same
Well done for you deserve it
So glad you found your fame

Well done to you all
For entertaining so well
Your production was ace

Tip
The place can
be changed to
suit the situation,
e.g. Broadway or
somewhere
else.

Lights, camera, action, quiet on set
A new star emerging, not one to forget
Success now awaits, you have travelled far
Step out into the limelight now you are a
STAR

BRAVO, BRAVO, BRAVO

May this great day
Live in your memory
With countless others
As your parents we are
So proud of all that
You have achieved
In your lifetime

Our warmest wishes as you
Represent your constituency
They could not have chosen
A better candidate for the job

We knew that you were special
So different from the rest
You have surpassed all the others
Everyone is so impressed
Now accolades are mounting
Praise and commendations
So proud of you our hero
Our heartfelt congratulations

Congratulations

Congratulations

So glad that you were chosen
To be in the team and play
You were all so very good
Go and celebrate the day
WELL DONE

Chosen for your country
How marvellous to know
The nation is behind you
Everywhere you must go
So fly the flag with pride
In all the things you do
Reach for those medals
Waiting there for you

Just to say...
So glad your
training paid off
And you won the race

Competition was tough
But you showed them all
That the trophy was yours
So its time to stand tall
We are so proud of you
That we could just burst
Well done to you now
For coming in first

HURRAY

We knew you were a winner
For your style and swing are great
The golfing trophy bears your name
So it is time to celebrate

Congratulations

Congratulations

May you always be a careful driver
Congratulations
On passing your test

Son, really glad you
passed your test
Now YOU can be
MY taxi service

Congratulations
well overdue
Saw you driving
your new car
Could not believe
it was you
Hope that you will
travel far

May you drive
With consideration
Always drive with care
Although the test is over
Your experience starts here

I suppose now
you have passed your test
My poor car will never get a rest

Fantastic news you passed the test
Now you are as good as all the rest

Congratulations

Congratulations

Congratulations

A first day at school for you
Full of friends and lots of fun
Enjoy everything that you do
School days have just begun

*W*ell goodness how swell you look
All dressed in school uniform
Have a happy time on your first day

Tip
Can change to
first day
at secondary
school etc.

As your child starts school

Lined up in the school yard
All of them waiting in a row
So amazing where time goes
How fast your children grow
Just think of all the fun times
With all the friends they find
Try not to worry too much
They will keep Mum in mind

Just to say...
Teachers like you are
hard to find
And difficult to
forget

How big are you,
our darling Son
Your first day at school
We hope you have fun

Only fools waste time and lose
Valuable information given
Them in their school days
Success lies before you
All you have to do is
Listen and learn
To everything
They offer
YOU

Sending you Good Luck
And wishing that you
Get the results you seek
They are long overdue
With all that hard work
You deserve the best

Congratulations on
your place
At a great new school
WELL DONE

All of the threads of life
Are being woven into place
Learn all you can at school
Make the world a better place

Just to say...
Well done on passing
your exams
It was worth all
the hard work

Treasure your schooldays
They are the first step
On the long road
To success
In life

Congratulations

Congratulations

Congratulations

117

My goodness me
I did not recognise you
In that graduation cap
All grown up now
WELL DONE GRADUATE

Just to say...
So proud to see those
letters after your name

Seems like only yesterday
Standing at the school gate
For your first day at school
But now you will graduate

Where did all the years go
The trials and tribulations
So confident and grown up
My sincere congratulations
ON GRADUATION DAY

I remember your first day at school
So clearly darling, we were both in tears
And here we stand on Graduation Day
So proud of you, both in tears of joy
Nothing much changes in our lives
Especially not our love and admiration
As your proud and very lucky parents

Celebrate, 'til the hour is late
It's not everyday you become a doctor

*A*s you pass out on parade
Marching proud in formations
A soldier now, our brave son

Just to say...
Lesser mortals would
have given up
Well done for
staying the course

When you were small I wondered

What it was that you would be

To make me so proud of you

Our son in the Royal Navy

Be brave, be bold, be daring

As you set sail upon the sea

For God will be there with you

And bring you safely home to me

Glad you finally worked out left from right Now you have joined the army

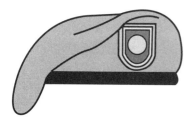

May the force be with you As you fly to foreign lands For your country

The uniform suits you, well done We are very proud of you

Tip
'Uniform' could be changed to 'cap and gown' for a student.

Friends & Family

To Mum

Over the years we have both changed so much

But something that has remained constant, Mum

Is my love for you and everything you do

To make my life as happy as can be

HAPPY MOTHER'S DAY

Everything you have ever done for me
And my family has always been
With love and affection
You're a Mum without compare
So very, very glad you care

MUM
Every day
In every way
You always
Colour
My life
With
LOVE

You're my Mum
My angel, my best friend
The one on whom I can depend
You're in my heart, my soul, my mind
A mother so loving, generous and kind
Not only on this special day but always
MAY YOU HAVE A TRULY
WONDERFUL DAY MUM

Just to say...
Sending smiles
across the miles
Have a really
lovely day Mum

Without you Mum
Nothing would be possible
Without you in my life loving me
Nothing would be important
Without your love
I would not be

HAPPY MOTHER'S DAY

MOTHER

Such a small word

That does not convey

The person who makes

My whole world a place

Where I feel so secure

Loved and protected

By someone who

Never lets me

Feel lost

Ever

Tip

This shaped verse could be used for Christmas or birthdays too.

Mum I just want to say
How much you mean to me
And how I really appreciate
Everything you've done for me

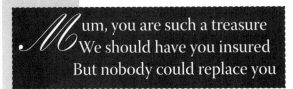

*M*um, you are such a treasure
We should have you insured
But nobody could replace you

I hope that on this Mother's Day
You'll have some time for 'You'
To do some of those special things
You have always wanted to

Just to say...
You are such a lovely
Step-Mum
And I love you so

It seems like only yesterday
You wiped away my tears
Helped me grow, watched me play
What happened to those years
Now children I have of my own
And I'm content and happy too
With grandchildren who love me
And it's all because of you
You really started something
When you fell in love with Dad
You were the perfect parents
And for that I'm really glad
You mean the very world to me
So there is nothing more to say
Than I love you very much Mum
Have a happy Mother's Day

May this day
Mum, hold
memories
Of a family who
loves you so

Tip
This verse
could be
adapted for a
birthday.

You wait without question
For me to get ready
You drive without question
For me to be safe
You love without question
For me, always there
You are without question
For me so amazing
MY DAD – BEST IN THE WORLD

Just to say...
There are good men and
there are great men
It's so good to know a
great man like you

Dad, I owe you so much
One day, when I'm rich
I will make a payment
I promise you

HAPPY FATHER'S DAY

On Father's Day
I wish you love, happiness
And joy far beyond compare
Everything you have always given
To all of your family

Mum told me that before I was born
You had lots of hair and no wrinkles
Then, she said that the wrinkles are
From all the times I made you smile
And that she quite likes bald men
So DAD, you should be glad really
That I helped you mature nicely
Into the mellow guy we all love

Years may pass and age us
And memories fade away
Yet inside I'm still the child
That you sat upon your knee
Listening to stories and jokes
Happy days, may this be one for you

HAPPY FATHER'S DAY

DAD
A short name
For ease of use
When we need
To call for help
From a man who
Is always there
No matter what
A name that means
LOVE

Just to say...
Dad, the things you
say touch my heart

I always know you're there
No matter what befalls
Guarding and protecting
Whenever danger calls
Dad you are so very special
I may not always tell you so
How much I really love you
Somehow I think you know

HAPPY FATHER'S DAY

DAD – You're the man
Who is always there
Like a steady rock
Where I can go
Anytime
To hold
On to

*D*ad, if you didn't have me
You would have no laughter lines
And besides, dark hair would look
Silly on you at your age

As time passes for us
Know that you will be forever
In my heart, in my daily thoughts
That I will speak of your wise words
Telling my own grandchildren of days
Full of love, laughter and contentment

HAPPY GRANDPARENTS' DAY

GRANDPARENTS' DAY

On this day of special wishes
Grandparents rule the day
So this card comes full of kisses
May many more be on the way

Grandparents are so special
They fill your life with joy
Especially when you are
A little girl or boy

HAPPY GRANDPARENTS' DAY

All things are possible
But our grandparents
Make them easier
To achieve

No matter what our age
We never forget words
Spoken by our grandparents
When we were too young
To appreciate what parents
Were trying to tell us

I do not need a special day
To send my love to both of you
Grandparents so very special
In everything you say and do
In my heart you are forever
Important pieces of my life
Memories I will always treasure
A loving Grandpa and his dear wife

Granddads always weave
A special kind of magic
Into your everyday life
Just by being there

GRANDMA

Your support and caring too
Are such a loving part of you
You always have an open door
A special person that I adore
You're always there to talk to me
With loving arms, as it should be
Close to my heart you will stay
On this and every single day

HAPPY GRANDPARENTS' DAY

I always know
when I'm sad
That you will be
the first one
To make me smile
again
I love you Nan

When it comes to groovy grannies
You have them all beat, Nan

Friends don't need to speak every day
To know that they are always
In each other's thoughts
And close at heart
Always

HAPPY FRIENDS' DAY
Special friends such as you
Are so rare in life
That they must be sent by God
To colour our lives
With His love

Your smile is worth
A thousand words
Your loving touch
Comforts my soul
Your enduring love
Keeps me warm
You are a friend
Without compare

True friends are angels with
invisible wings
Blessing our lives with such
precious things

On this special day for friends
May the friendship you give to others
Be rewarded with love
May the love you give to others
Be treasured always
May all the joy you give to others
Be returned to you tenfold

Friends & Family

Friends & Family

You do not need a special date
If you just want to celebrate
Look at everything God gives you
That is the reason that it's due
Give a smile to everyone you meet
As you go walking down the street
For a smile is such a special thing
To touch a heart and make it sing
Share the love God gives for free
That I send now to you from me
HAPPY FRIENDS' EVERY DAY

Sending you a smile
To let you know
I'm thinking of you
Especially on Friends' Day

You really are a Special Friend
And you're sent a world of love
May you find the best of life ahead
And all that you are dreaming of
But on this day of friendship
Extra loving wishes you will find
For a friend worth more than gold
Who is never far from mind

Just to say...
Knowing you has been
one of life's true
miracles

May Friends' Day be as happy and joyful
As your precious friendship has made me

My lovely friend

Your thoughtfulness comes
As a gift from heaven above
Each day you colour my life
With your warm, caring love

My dear friend you are
A special gift from God
You fill my life with joy
Love beyond compare
I am so thankful that
You are always there
HAPPY FRIENDS' DAY

There is nothing more comforting
Than a dear friend in whom you can confide
So glad that we have connected
In heart, mind and soul

Thinking of you, my dear friend
Warms my heart and fills my
day with smiles
Reflections of days gone by
and those ahead
Knowing that I can share them
with you
Makes my world a brighter place
HAPPY FRIENDS' DAY

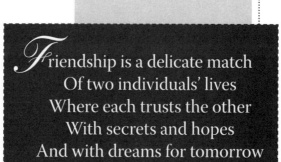

Friendship is a delicate match
Of two individuals' lives
Where each trusts the other
With secrets and hopes
And with dreams for tomorrow

Friends & Family
Friends & Family

Festive
Wishes

This Christmas light a candle
And thank God for the reason
For the season, His only Son

At this festive time of the year
Count your blessings and remember
Those who are not as fortunate as you
For they are also the children of God

May you awake
On the Christmas Morn
To find a Winter
Wonderland

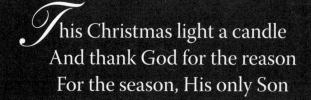

Tell me
How you know
What to buy a friend
On the birthday of Jesus
To show how much you care
For your friendship with them
LOVE-LOVE-LOVE-LOVE-LOVE
What do you give to a friend
Who is always there for you
When you are feeling low
Why this card of course
Filled with love
From me
HAPPY CHRISTMAS

Tip
This bauble-
shaped card can be
amended on lines 4
and 14 to use
for Easter as an
Easter egg.

*H*appy Kissmass

O
Lord
You gave
Your only Son, Jesus
to show the world how you
loved us so and we thank you now
in our hearts, thoughts and mind for being
there for us always in so many ways so that
we only need to ask you for help and you
will answer our humble prayers

May your house be filled with love
And thoughts of the real meaning of
Christmas

May every path we tread
This Christmas time
Lead us to peace

All the joy of the season
We are sending your way
May you feel Jesus around you
On this Christmas Day

So the love that He gives you
Fills your home with good cheer
Stays in your hearts on His birthday
And in the forthcoming New Year

May your family draw
near at Christmas
And be wrapped together
in the gift of love

May the spirit of Christmas
Fill you with joy
As you remember the manger
And a new little boy
Who was born just to save us
And to show us God's love
That surrounds and protects us
Shines down from above

Lead heavenly star
Towards a new tomorrow
Filled with love, peace and joy

On Christmas Day
May you find the child within you
Make it a magical time

Holly and tinsel
Soft white snow
Waiting for Santa
By fires that glow

Christmas wishes
to you
Hope the day is packed
with fun
In everything that
you do

Mum and Dad......

May happiness surround you

Upon the Christmas morn

A joyous time to celebrate

The day that He was born

With thanks from those around you

Who share this special day

We send this with our love to you

Because we want to say

You're extra special people

Who always bring good cheer

So have a very Merry Christmas

And a peaceful Happy New Year

Tip
The last four lines of the verse can stand alone.

You may not be my parents
But to me you're 'Mum and Dad'
So at this special time of year
It makes me really glad

To send to both of you my love
For all the years we've shared
You were truly sent from God above
The way you really cared

When I was down you picked me up
When sad, you made me smile
And if everything seemed lost to me
You went that extra mile

For everything you did for me
My love to both of you
Special thoughts for Christmas Day
And throughout your lifetime too

Hi-ho-hi-ho
Christmas Day
With snow
Santa snoring
Very boring
Hi-ho-hi-ho

God bless
Everyone in the world
With the joy of
CHRISTMAS

Wishing you love and happiness
At this holy time of year
A time for caring and sharing
With ones you hold dear

*M*ay Christmas bring
Old friends and new
With loving wishes
Just for you

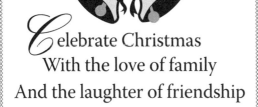

*C*elebrate Christmas
With the love of family
And the laughter of friendship

*M*istletoe and Holly
May your holiday be jolly

Wishing you every happiness
At Christmas
And throughout the coming
New Year

May your holiday be filled
With good friends and family
May the sound of laughter echo
Into the New Year

A special festive greeting
That brings a double share
Of love and deep affection
To a very special pair

Last Christmas was a bit of a blur
And the New Year was a bit of a fog
Try not to celebrate too much this year

Festive Wishes

Festive Wishes

Festive Wishes

Greetings of this lovely season
And extra special wishes too
For a truly wonderful Christmas
And a fun-filled New Year too

You are everything to me
At Christmas and always
I love you with all my heart

With you in my life every day is magical
Not just Christmas and the New Year
But every day that I see you smile
And hear you call my name
I love you so much

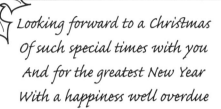

Looking forward to a Christmas
Of such special times with you
And for the greatest New Year
With a happiness well overdue

Enjoy the magic of
Christmas
Celebrate with friends of
good cheer
So that a special kind of
spirit
Follows you into the
New Year

Christmas is a time for giving
So I'm sending you all my love
I'm hoping that what you get is
What you've been dreaming of
For you put such a dedication
Into everything that you do
If anyone deserves success
My darling, then it is you

Festive Wishes

Santa Claus has a treat
To bring just for you
For you are so special
In everything you do

You are my special
Christmas Cracker
My love, my peace, my joy

All those awful Christmas presents
That you never really need
Give them to a charity shop
As your New Year good deed

Just to say...
It's not a rumour
It's really true
All I want for
Christmas
Is you

On Christmas Eve know
That I am thinking of you
On Christmas Day know
That love surrounds you
On New Year's Day know
That you are in my heart

Mistletoe and holly
All the joy of the season
A time to share love
For a very special reason

Festive Wishes

Festive Wishes

Festive Wishes

A letter to Santa......

We are writing to ask you, as good girls and boys
If, in your big sack, you might find us some toys
But also dear Santa we would like you to send
Hugs, loves and kisses to our family and friends
And if you might find, on a cold Christmas Day
Some soft, fluffy snow could you send it our way
So the magic of Christmas will spread all around
In a carpet of love that will cover the ground

Santa's sack is full of toys for you
Listen for him on Christmas Eve
When you see his gifts for you
Then you truly will believe

A reply from Santa......

Santa found your letter
And it filled his heart with joy
To receive a special little note
From such lovely girls and boys

He said you'd asked for kisses
For those who you love so
And for extra special wishes
For a Christmas Day with snow

When it came to asking Santa
For some presents he did say
That he's granted all your wishes
Look for them on Christmas Day

Tip
This verse could be used for scrapbooking or a special project at Christmas.

*M*ay your first Christmas
Be as wonderful as you are
Little angel

1st Christmas

May this first Christmas bring
You His love and warmth
To make this a truly
Wonderful Day
For you to
Treasure
Always

Baby's 1st Christmas

Celebrate the birth of love
On your first Christmas Day
As we praise His name

May the true meaning of
Christmas
Surround you as you celebrate
For the first time

Santa got my message
To stop by your house
If you hear him coming
Be quiet as a mouse
He has something special
To leave by your tree
Wrapped up with love
Especially from me

Happy 1st Christmas

Sitting in the sun, with a cocktail
In hand and an ice cream melting
It does not feel like Christmas Day
But then it does feel like heaven

MERRY CHRISTMAS AND A HOT
NEW YEAR

Just to say...
Miles keeps us
distant, love keeps us
close at heart

Looking forward to a celebration
All of our own when you return
To your loving family soon
HAPPY CHRISTMAS

Travelling across the miles just to be there
I have everything I want for Christmas
A special holiday time with you
Sharing all the joy and love
The season brings
See you soon

The magic of Christmas
Is making loved ones
Feel closer even though
They are miles apart

From our house in the UK
A friendly card, just to say
Wherever you may roam
It won't feel like Christmas
'Til you are back home

Tip
You can change the UK to USA, or elsewhere.

Dates to
Celebrate

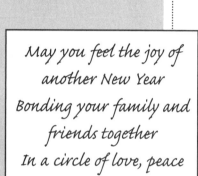

New Year

With each new year comes hope
This year make every day count
By taking one step each day
On a journey of kindness
Love and compassion
Towards your fellow man
Look back at the close of day
And know you made a difference

May you feel the joy of
another New Year
Bonding your family and
friends together
In a circle of love, peace
and happiness

Just a little note to say
How happy you make me
A special friend I treasure
And you will always be
Close in my thoughts forever
Because you always care
Here's to the coming year
And moments we will share

May the New Year
Begin with a bang
To colour your life
With good fortune

May the coming New Year
Bring you good luck, good health
And happiness knocking at your door

Just to say...
Let go of yesterdays
and capture
tomorrow's
dreams

For every mile
between us
I send you a sweet kiss
Not long 'til we
are together
The New Year will
be bliss

May
the New Year
Be the one for you
Where your special hopes
And dearest dreams come true

No present this Christmas
Just a card filled with love
But a New Year surprise
That's all that you dream of

*D*on't drink too much at
Christmas
You will miss the
New Year Celebrations

May the forthcoming New Year
Be filled with the very best
Of everything for you

Christmas will not be the same
Without you here to open the presents
But New Year will be fantastic
Because you'll be here celebrating with us

May your holiday dreams come true
And may the memories last
The whole year through

All of our thoughts are with you
At this season of goodwill and cheer
May you all enjoy this holiday time
And find joy in the coming New Year

Here's wishing your first Easter
With your new baby
Is full of laughter and smiles

Glad I have somebunny special
To share my Easter eggs with
For you make me so happy

*S*ending you fond wishes
For a Blessed Easter

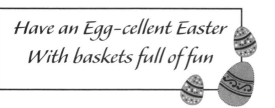

Have an Egg-cellent Easter
With baskets full of fun

Sending you my wishes
for a springtime
fresh with new promises
And an Easter time filled
with hope and happiness

New love, new life, new beginnings

Sending you warm wishes
For a beautiful spring season

A rainbow of ribbons
Hear children sing
Dance round the maypole
To herald in spring
Crown one of beauty
As May Queen that day
Chase all the bleakness
Of winter away

Celebrate the life
Of St John the Baptist
This Midsummer's Day
Give thanks and rejoice
For all he gave to us
So that we could love God
As He should be loved
With all our heart

Enjoy the magic of Midsummer's Eve
As we await the longest day of the year
Celebrate love, life and happiness
For you are one of God's children
And He will always be in your heart
As He walks beside you in life

Creatures of the darkest night
On all hallows eve are beckoning you
Dress up well and look a fright
And bring some spirits too

All dressed up in costume
We will be such a sight
Our Halloween Party will
Be a great fright night

Come all you ghosts and witches
You frightful creatures of night
Dracula is having a monster party
So do come round for a bite

Join us if you dare
For a night of trick or treat
That's sure to scare

We plough the fields
And scatter the good seed
So we can enjoy a harvest of plenty

All things bright and beautiful

God gave all of them to us

Give thanks, praise Him

For His harvest

Just to say...

Live everyday God
gives you as He
would want
you to

May the Lord
Guide you and walk with you
On your Holy Path of Glory
Congratulations
On your
ORDINATION

May your faith in the Lord
Be reaffirmed
On your confirmation

Wishing you
An easy fast on
YOM KIPPUR

Wishing you and
your loved ones
A Blessed month of
Tishri

May God bless you and your family
With enough to be thankful to Him
Have a Blessed Sukkot

May
The Torah
Bless you
Inspire you
And guide you
Today and always
Congratulations
On your
Bar Mitzvah

*M*azel Tov
On becoming a Bar Mitzvah
Wishing you joy today
and always

MUBARAK

My dear friend

As the crescent moon is sighted

And the Holy month of Ramadan begins

May Allah bless your family with happiness

And grace your home with peace and warmth

ISLAM
EID AL-FITTR
May the blessings of Allah
Be with you at Eid Al-Fittr
Bringing joy to your heart

AL-HIJRA
As you herald
in another year
May it bring
good fortune
Love and prosperity
to you and
your loved ones

*M*ay
Allah's Rahmat
Be showered on you
At this Holy time

From their pure love
Of family and African culture
Build a firm foundation
For your family and community
Respect your identity
Harmonize with others
And be true to your heritage
Not just at Kwanzaa
But each and every day

HAPPY KWANZAA

May the Guru dwell
In you and bless your soul
With eternal peace and harmony

Wishing you
And your family
Love and comfort on
BAISHAKHI

*M*ay the Lord Buddha
Bless you in every step you take

SAINT ANDREW

White cross where he died
Upon the day that Christians cried
A disciple who spread the word
So Christianity could be heard
Blue for the sky above his head
Remember all the words he said
Celebrate his life and pray
For him upon St Andrew's Day

May St David's Day
Bring love, joy and peace to
your home
As you wear your daffodil
With Welsh pride and dignity

On St Patrick's Day

May the wings of a butterfly kiss the sun
And find your shoulder to linger on
Bringing you luck beyond compare
And great happiness for you to share
With those people of whom you're fond
Today, tomorrow and far beyond

*W*ear St George's colours with pride
Upon the day this Christian died

HAPPY THANKSGIVING
For a bountiful harvest
All around the world celebrate
Erntedank – Dayak – Onam
Maras Taun - Chuseok – Dongmaeng
Pongal – Solung – Sukkot – Timoleague
Makar Sankranti – Gawai Dayak - Sabah
Ikore – Vaisakhi – Nabanna - Kaamantan
THE HARVEST FESTIVAL

THANKSGIVING
A time to count
Our blessings
I'm grateful to be blessed
With you and all the
Bountiful love
You create
In my life

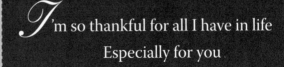

I'm so thankful for all I have in life
Especially for you

Happy Independence Day
Celebrate in style by giving to
Your fellow man the gift
Of a simple smile

Celebrate
A new beginning
On Bastille Day

FRENCH VERSION
Célébrez
Un nouveau commencement
Le jour de Bastille

Suppliers

UK Wholesalers

Crafts Too Ltd
Unit 2 Kingstons Industrial Estate
Eastern Road
Aldershot
Hants GU12 4YA
Tel: (+44) (0)1252 330024
www.crafts-too.com
*Wholesaler of craft products
importing and distributing
ranges from USA & Europe*

Design Objectives
www.docrafts.co.uk
*Contact them directly through
the website or contact Magna
Craft on 01730 815555*

Personal Impressions
Curzon Road
Chiltern Industrial Estate
Sudbury
Suffolk CO10 2XW
Tel: (+44) (0)1787 375241
www.richstamp.co.uk
*Visit website or call for your
nearest stockists of their craft
products from USA & UK.
Importers of products listed in
USA section*

Pergamano UK
Curzon Road
Chiltern Industrial Estate
Sudbury
Suffolk CO10 2XW
Tel: (+44) (0)1787 375241
www.richstamp.co.uk
*Sole UK importer of Pergamano
Parchment Craft Products.
Contact for your nearest
Pergamano tutor and retailer*

UK Retailers

Arty and Crafty Supplies
Genestic Cottage
Monkton
Honiton
Devon EX14 9QH
www.buycraftsonline.co.uk
*Online art and craft retailer
specialising in card making
– sorry no personal callers.
Retailers of products from
Personal Impressions and
Pergamano UK*

Craft Creations
Ingersoll House
Delamere Road
Cheshunt
Hertfordshire
EN8 9HD
Tel: (+44) (0)1992 781900
www.craftcreations.co.uk
*Greeting card blanks and
general craft retailer. Mail order
or contact for stockists*

Craftwork Cards Ltd
Unit 2, The Moorings
Waterside Road
Stourton
Leeds
West Yorkshire
LS10 1RW
Tel: 0113 276 5713
www.craftworkcards.com
*Sell greetings cards blanks and
other specialist card making
materials. Mail order available,
but visit the shop for the full
range of supplies*

Fred Aldous Ltd
37 Lever Street
Manchester
M1 1LW
Tel: (+44) (0)161 326 2477
www.fredaldous.co.uk
Originally established in 1886, this is an Aladdin's Cave of art and craft materials with craft workshops available there too

Hobbycraft Stores
Tel: 0800 027 2387
www.hobbycraft.co.uk
General craft retailer countrywide. Mail order available or call for your nearest store

Paper Cellar Ltd
Langley Place
99 Langley Road
Watford
Hertfordshire
WD17 4AU
Tel: 0871 871 3711
www.papercellar.com
Specialize in paper products, including card making materials. Buy online or visit website for nearest stockist

USA

The ranges of craft products listed here are imported into the UK by Personal Impressions see the UK listing for contact details

American Traditional Designs
442 First NH Turnpike.
Northwood
NH 03261
Tel: 1-800-448-6656
www.americantraditional.com
Embossing stencil manufacturers. Visit the website for details of products and local stockists

Artistic Wire Limited
752 North Larch Avenue
Elmhurst
IL 60126
Tel: 630-530-7567
www.artisticwire.com
View a full range of wires and accessories and locate your nearest stockist from the website

Art Institute Glitter
712 N Balboa Street
Cottonwood
Arizona
86326
Tel: toll free [877] 909-0805
www.artglitter.com
Projects, products and a gallery online with details of suppliers in your area

Magic Mesh
PO Box 8
Lake City
MN55041
Tel: 651-345-6374
www.magicmesh.com
Full range of products, project ideas for card making and scrapbooking, with stockist list

Ranger Industries Inc
15 Park Road
Tinton Falls
NJ 07724
Tel: 732-389-3535
www.rangerink.com
Visit website to see vast range of products for rubber stamping

Suppliers

Tsukineko, Inc
17640 NE 65th Street
Redmond, WA 98052 USA
Tel: (425) 883-7733
www.tsukineko.com
Manufacturers of unique ink products and craft accessories that fire your imagination

Uchida Of AmericaCorp
3535 Del Amo Boulevard
Torrance
CA 90503
Tel: 1-800-541-5877
www.uchida.com
Manufacturers of art and craft materials for card making, scrapbooking and art projects

USArtQuest Inc
7800 Ann Arbor Road
Grass Lake
MI 49240
Tel: 517-522-6225
www.usartquest.com
Visit the website for tips and techniques to help you with your arts and crafts projects

Europe

Kars Creative Wholesale
Industriweg 27
Industrieterrein 'De Heuning'
Postbus 97
4050 EB Ochten
The Netherlands
Tel: (+31) (0) 344 642864
www.kars.nl
Visit website or call for your nearest stockists of Pergamano and other craft products

JEJE Produkt V.O.F.
Verlengde Zuiderloswal 12
1216 BX Hilversum
The Netherlands
Tel: 035 624 6732
www.jejeprodukt.nl
Suppliers of Sandy Art product range, stickers and ahesive products

Pergamano International
Postbus 86
1420 AB Uithoorn
The Netherlands
Tel: (+31) (0) 297 526256
www.pergamano.com
Parchment craft manufacturers. Visit website for product information or nearest stockists

Australia

ParchCraft Australia
PO Box 1026
Elizabeth Vale
South Australia 5112
www.parchcraftaustralia.com
View metal parchment craft tools on website

Canada

Magenta Rubber Stamps
2275 Bombbardier Street
Sainte-Julie
Quebec J3H 3B4
Tel: 450-922-5253
www.magentastyle.com

South Africa

Brasch Hobby
10 Loveday Street South
Selby
Johannesburg
South Africa 2001
Tel: +27 11 493 9100
www.brasch.co.za
Manufacturers and distributors of genuine heritage craft products

About the Author
Judith Wibberley

Born and bred in Cheshire, she moved to Manchester when she married Colin. After raising their children, James and Deborah, she opened an arts and crafts centre specializing in handmade cards where her love of creative writing lead to these verses especially for card makers. Although she will always be a Northern Lass, Judith Wibberley now resides in the beautiful Otter Valley in Monkton, Devon with her husband, where she writes and runs a craft website www.buycraftsonline.co.uk and Writers Website www.judithwibberley.co.uk

Index